How to Fight Depression – (Booklet)
9 Case Studies

John F. Walsh, M.S.
And
Joyce Zborower, M.A.

ISBN = 1492920193

ISBN-13 = 978-1492920199

Table of Contents

How to Fight Depression – (Booklet)
With 9 Case Studies

"What Is Depression?"

When somebody suffers from depression, it is more than just feeling blue, or sad, or down in the dumps. It is a life-altering feeling which can leave a person a mere shell of her former self.

Depression can completely decimate a person and can affect him/her in such a negative way that she often finds she has no will left to survive. But it is also more than just a horrible feeling of giving up. When you ask "What is depression?" it's important to understand it is an actual medical condition.

Signs Of Depression

Depression can manifest itself any number of ways, but the most frequent manifestations include:
-- loss if interest in activities which used to be enjoyable
-- fatigue
-- loss of appetite
-- sleeping a lot
-- and lack of motivation.

While these symptoms are rather vague, when taken overall with a person's feeling of lack of overall well-being, they can be a strong indicator of depression. Though there are specific tests to help with diagnosis, a doctor will usually just listen to the symptoms and begin treatment with medication and/or counseling.

Causes Of Depression

There could be a variety of factors causing someone to be depressed. These could include genetic predisposition, or environmental, psychological, and/or biochemical factors. It affects every person differently, but many of the symptoms are similar from case to case.

The genetic link to depression has only recently been discovered. This was a huge breakthrough in this malady's study and treatment. Geneticists have discovered an abnormality on chromosome 15 for one or both of the parents which can be passed down to a child. This can lead to that child's depression later on in life.

Environmental factors can also play a huge role in depression. Studies of Seasonal Affective Disorder, also known as SAD, show that when people see less of the sun, such as what occurs in winter months or in certain regions of the country that consistently have less sunshine, people are more likely to become depressed. This shows that the sun's light can have a huge impact on whether or not a person may or may not become depressed.

Psychological factors also contribute to depression in some people. Psychological factors can be described as anything that changes your overall mood or mental state. A death in the family. Witnessing something scary. Having any type of traumatic experience. These and any number of other psychological triggers can precipitate depression..

Biochemical factors are the biggest contributors of frequent and continuous depression in people. There is a misfiring of chemicals in a person's brain which can contribute to dopamine receptors in the brain not receiving the proper signals. When this happens, a person can suffer from frequent and chronic depression.

Let's look a little closer at the environmental factors.

Seasonal Depression: Symptoms, Causes, Treatments

Seasonal Depression is also known by a variety of other names like Seasonal Affective Disorder (SAD), winter blues, summer blues, etc. This is a recurring pattern tending to show up year after year. As the name suggests, in each year, at one specific season/time, an individual may find him/herself with a depressive episode while for the rest of the year he/she is in a normal emotional state.

The most commonly seen seasonal depression starts during the fall and continues through the winter months -- improving with the start of sunny days in spring/summer. This pattern is called 'Winter Depression'. It is more commonly seen in women and in Western Countries where sunlight is present for a very short time during winter months and where there is wide variation in daylight availability during various seasons.

During the winter season, even in other species, activity level is decreased owing to decreased availability of food as well as survival difficulties of the cold weather. Think about bears. Hibernation is an extreme example of avoiding the cold weather.

Depression starting in the months of spring or summer is rare and is known as 'Summer Depression'.

As the particular season begins, the symptoms of depression are mild but gradually worsen as the season progresses. An individual may start feeling very moody, not find interest in any activity, his/her energy levels start to drop. He gets easily tired, becomes anxious and irritable over minor things, tends to withdraw from social activities and lacks concentration for doing any work. Lastly, feelings of hopelessness and worthlessness overpower him and he may start getting thoughts of death or ideas of suicide.

Those with winter depression tend to oversleep with daytime drowsiness and napping, overeat with cravings of high carbohydrate content food like pastas, cheese, bread, etc. leading to weight gain and lethargy. They also start having heavy or 'leaden'(lead like) feelings in their arms and legs, prefer to be alone and become socially withdrawn while those with summer onset have more irritability, difficulty in sleeping, loss of appetite and thus weight loss and occasionally increased sexual drive.

Causes
The exact cause of this seasonal depression is not yet known, but according to experts, because of its frequent occurrence during winter months, certain chemical changes in the brain occur depending on the availability of sunlight. Also the variation in the chemical melatonin secreted by the pineal gland in darkness or dim light may play a role.

The decreased sunlight during winter months may disturb the body's internal biological clock (circadian rhythm) or cause a decrease in the serotonin neurotransmitter levels in the brain and thus lead to depression. As it occurs more commonly in those who live in regions away from the equator leading to decreased exposure to natural sunlight and also in those having a family history of depression or other mood disorders, certain familial, genetic and geographic factors may also have a role in its causation.

Diagnosis
The diagnosis of this condition is mainly by a thorough evaluation of the symptoms by an experienced health care professional. Also maintaining of a diary and noting down all of one's symptoms and the time of the year when they are usually present and also the presence of any major life changes or stressors or any medication one is taking can help the doctor in formulating a proper diagnosis. There are no other medical or blood tests for making the diagnosis.

Treatment
The treatment of seasonal depression mainly includes a combination of antidepressant medications, psychotherapy and most importantly light therapy or phototherapy.

In phototherapy the individual is exposed to bright light in the range of 1500-10,000 lux by sitting in front of a light box that's on a table or desk for about 1-2 hours before dawn every morning or after dusk in the evening. This is known as bright light treatment.

Another treatment technique, known as dawn simulation, consists of a dim light that is put on automatically early in the morning when one is sleeping and it starts getting brighter over time, simulating a sunrise.

With light therapy, symptoms start to improve within 3-4 days with no serious side effects.

Various antidepressants like paroxetine, sertraline, fluoxetine, venlafaxine and bupropion may also be helpful in alleviating seasonal depression.

Certain household remedies or natural treatments for this condition include regular exposure to sunlight by opening the blinds or windows and allowing the light to come into the house or office, taking a walk outside in the park or gardens and regular physical exercise and relaxation to relive anxiety and stress. Taking short vacations during the months of depression to places where the season is better to one's condition is also helpful.

Biochemical factors associated with depression vary, but two of the most important here are depressions associated with pregnancy and depressions associated with brain chemical dysfunctions, i.e. bipolar disorder. We'll look at each of these next.

What Exactly Is Postpartum Depression?

Postpartum depression is a type of clinical depression seen in women who have just delivered a baby. It is treatable and the symptoms can be alleviated.

What Causes Postpartum Depression?

No one really knows for sure, but current speculation has it that PPD results from the sudden decrease in progesterone following giving birth. For this reason, hormone replacement therapy is often the treatment of choice for getting rid of the symptoms.

Another cause could be the stress levels that rise during and after the pregnancy. Prior to the birth, the woman had much more freedom and many fewer responsibilities. Babies tend to restrict your behavior. You can no longer do what you want when you want as the baby's needs must always come first. This can lead to some resentment towards the baby – especially amongst younger new mothers.

What Are The symptoms?

Many of the symptoms of postpartum depression are the same as other types of depression: sadness, low self-esteem, a tendency toward isolation, frequent crying – sometimes for no apparent reason.

Oftentimes the mother will have thoughts of hurting the baby or herself. Such thoughts tend to produce overwhelming feelings of guilt. And the quilt tends to lower her self-esteem even more leading to very negative self-talk and self-recriminations.

Other symptoms include irritability, trouble sleeping and/or a loss of appetite.

How To Cure Postpartum Depression

There are many treatments available, both natural and medical. Natural treatments are generally reserved for the mild forms of this condition and mainly consist of various herbs. One of the great benefits of natural depressive treatments is their lack of side effects. They are also fairly cost-effective.

Medical treatments for this condition generally include some type of antidepressant either alone or in conjunction with hormone replacement therapy or counseling. For extreme cases, antipsychotic medication or electroconvulsive therapy may be recommended.

Many people who struggle with this type of depression find that a social support group and many friends can help them better cope with their situation.

Postpartum depression is extremely difficult to go through, especially for women who have no idea about how to cure the problem, but with the right help getting to the other side is definitely doable.

And this brings us to bipolar depression, also called manic depression.

What is Manic Depression?

Manic depression is a term used historically for what is now better known as 'Bipolar Disorder', 'Bipolar Affective Disorder' or 'Bipolar Mood Disorder'. All these terms refer to the same brain chemical disorder in which there are unusual shifts in one's mood, energy levels, thought processes (cognition) and the ability to perform one's day-to-day tasks The individual's mood alternates between the poles of depression (lows) and mania (highs) leading to unusual and sometimes dramatic 'mood swings' and bizarre behavior.

A healthy individual also experiences a wide range of moods which keep fluctuating daily but are proportional to the circumstances that provoke them. One may feel sad or low when scolded by a parent or senior, may feel quite happy or high if when receiving a gift or compliment and then may come back to normal. These things happen in lives daily.

When normal fluctuations in mood become very extreme, it is called as manic depression. The various daily human experiences are exaggerated to larger than life proportions. Normal sadness or fatigue or even joy and happiness, energy and creativity are carried to extremes. Normal thought processes, motivation, behavior, physiology as well as psycho-social functioning can be affected adversely.

Results can be seen in damaged relationships, poor school or job performance and even harming oneself or others. But the condition can be treated and the individual with the illness can lead a full and productive life.

Generally one has the control over his/her feelings and mood, but when this sense of control is lost, and there is a subjective experience of great distress, it becomes a disorder which requires medical attention and treatment.

The mood swings in manic depression may range from being very mild to a very extreme and they may happen either gradually or suddenly within a timeframe of even minutes to hours. When these mood swings happen frequently and too fast it is called as 'rapid cycling'. A milder form of this disorder is called 'cyclothymia', and when the disorder follows a specific seasonal pattern, it is called 'seasonal affective disorder'.

The symptoms of manic-depressive illness are classified according to a depressive episode, a manic episode or a mixed episode.

The most common symptoms during a depressive episode include a pessimistic, bleak and despairing mood, a deep sense of futility, inability to experience pleasure in any activities, sleep and appetite disturbances, feelings of guilt, hopelessness, worthlessness and, at the extreme, ideas of suicide.

Some of the common symptoms during a manic episode include heightened mood, faster speech and speed of doing things, quicker thoughts racing through the mind, increased creativity, a decreased need for sleep, easy irritability, increased sexuality and impulsivity. Also the individual may spend a lot of money, make foolish investments or start a new business or multiple businesses at the same time, may get involved in foolish partnerships or may even make lots of donations due to the loss of his/her judgment power.

During a mixed episode, symptoms of mania and depression occur together and often include difficulty sleeping, agitation, marked changes in appetite and suicidal thoughts. One may feel very sad or hopeless and at the very same time feel extremely energized.

In some of the more severe episodes of the disorder, psychotic symptoms may also be present like delusions or hallucinations.

The exact cause of the manic depressive disorder is yet to be found but it is known that various neurotransmitters in the brain -- like serotonin, epinephrine, nor-epinephrine and dopamine --play an important role in the causation. Various hormones like thyroid, prolactin and growth hormone also have a role. This disorder tends to run in families which has lead to identifying certain genes which increase the risk of inheriting the disorder.

With advances in the field of brain scanning, the areas of the brain involved in this disorder are being identified.

There are a wide variety of treatment options available for mood disorders but they need to be individualized according to one's type, circumstances, symptoms, age and presence of other medical problems. Also, as this disorder is currently thought of as a lifetime illness with recurrent episodes and a high risk of suicide, the opinion and consultation of a mental health professional is a must for all those experiencing major mood changes.

There are many other depression types, some of which will be touched on in the following case studies. For now, however, I think the above gives you a fairly clear picture of the highlights of this disease. The case studies will take you deeper than, maybe you even want to go.

Case Studies in Depression

By John F. Walsh, M.S.

Jack F. Walsh, M.S.
1937 – 2012

Following two years working for the Daytona, Fla Police Department Jack Walsh received his master degree in clinical psychology from Bradley University.

While taking a master class in Rorschach (ink blot test) taught by Samuel Beck, one of the three top names in Rorschach interpretation, he was invited to attend the University of Chicago PhD program. He elected, instead to spend at least one year in every phase of mental health treatment available. This includes a 7000 bed hospital outside of Chicago, a center for special needs children in North Carolina, Director of a Model Cities program in Charlotte, N.C., forensics training in Columbia, SC leading to his certification as non medical forensic examiner for the state of South Carolina, just to name a few.

Jack is an award winning photographer whose photo essay on the Chicago riots was featured by The Business Executives Against the Vietnamese War. He continued sending photographs of conflicts from Chicago, Prague, East and West Berlin, Belfast and Londonderry. He has currently authored his first book, published posthumously, Emergency Services Mental Health Professional - Memoirs and Experiences [Kindle Edition] which covers forty five years of our history as seen from a satirical eye. It is available from Amazon.com.

"What Does Depression Feel Like?"

"I don't like standing near the edge of a platform when an express train is passing through. I like to stand right back and if possible get a pillar between me and the train. I don't like to stand by the side of a ship and look down into the water. A second's action would end everything. A few drops of desperation." - Winston Churchill (1874-1965)

(Names and places have been changed to protect privacy.)

In everyone's life there are periods of "what's the use"? But clouds recede and optimism returns ... for most people. I'd like to introduce you to three of my clients. Two are dealing with the consequences of depression and one has a different agenda.

Diana works for the telephone company manning the computer. She has two sisters and two brothers. Her father is a lineman in North Carolina. Her mother and the other sons and daughters live in Palm Beach County, Florida. Diana lives in Charlotte. NC. She has a boyfriend whom she is afraid of. She smokes marijuana and has been known to take pills.

Don is in his late 20's. My major contact with him is when he is brought into the emergency room following self inflicted knife wounds. He is a single child not much is known about his parents as he lives alone. These episodes seem to occur about once every two months. When these events happen he is usually accompanied by a different distraught girlfriend. Don is unemployed.

Bob is a master's chess player. He lives with his family. He is well spoken, conservatively dressed and in his second year of college. He is not currently in a relationship. He feels like an outcast on occasion as his interest in classical music, especially chamber music, is not shared by his peers. On occasion he works with his father's catering service but has little interest in following this line of work.

I received an emergency phone call that Diana was freaking out. I went to the second floor apartment she shared with her girlfriend. There were two girls and four guys smoking opiated hash with discordant music blasting. Everyone in the living room seemed oblivious to any emergency, and pretty much oblivious to anything but the hash, in my opinion.

The girl friend who made the call ushered me into the bedroom where Diana was having a meltdown. Feeling that Johnny Rotten and the Sex Pistols did not contribute to a calm ambiance I was seeking so I shouted to shut the damn thing off. I might have had better luck discussing proportional representation with a herd of grazing cattle, so I just pulled the cord out of the wall. Diana was shivering, sitting on the floor with her arms hugging her knees. She was aware of me being there and seemed mortified that I saw her in this condition. I helped her up and we left the apartment. Approaching the stairs Diana exploded into resistance causing us both to tumble down the concrete steps. I shielded her head from making contact. I admitted her to the psychiatric wing of the local hospital.

Another emergency call from a hysterical woman. Don had set himself on fire and was sitting in his car in the hospital parking lot. The fire department had arrived and Don had received minor burns to his chest and arms. There was an added issue. Apparently there was a bomb in the trunk of the car. That involved the local police and representatives from Shaw Air Force Base Bomb Squad. Standing around the hospital parking lot waiting for the bomb to go off was the hospital administer, three firemen, four cops, myself and a screaming girlfriend.

The bomb experts from Shaw asked who was in charge? "Well that kinda depends on just which level of authority you might consider", I thought to myself and pointed to the senior police officer. The bomb squad elected to drive the car back to Shaw, the firemen folded their hoses and left, the cops left leaving one to fill out the incident report. The hospital administer was relieved that a bomb didn't go off in the hospital parking lot, the girl had now stopped screaming and Don was back on the psych unit.

Bob was having a bad day. He had been up three nights straight, wouldn't eat and kept perseverating on Kasparov pawn B-5. He got into the family car and drove off and it wasn't until 14 hours later that he was located at a truck stop 300 miles away, crying. He was admitted to a local hospital, given a sedative and kept under observation.

Diana looked out the meshed screened fourth floor window at a girl getting into her automobile and thought to herself, "I really am crazy!" She was taken for a series of twelve electro shock treatments (EST). She described her experience following her first day back to work.

"It was weird. I would open a drawer and see a sweater. It had to be mine but I've never seen it before. At work I had a little trouble remembering which floor my office was located. Kathy a co-worker greeted me. I know she has children but I can't remember their names. It's like you have to concentrate so hard putting the pieces together you don't have time to feel depressed."

Don had little recollection of what happened. Because every time we are called he is so slobbering drunk that we could never get any useful information about him. Even in moments of rare sobriety his answers were vague and incoherent. He did recognize me and regarded me in a positive light. His chest and arms had so many cut scars that he looked like an AAA road map. It was his twelfth hospital admission.

Bob had been noncompliant with his bi-polar medication. He explained, "It's like everything was so clear I understood everything." I asked him what Kasparov pawn B-5 was about. He explained that in Kasparov vs. Topalov, 1999 one of the most outstanding chess matches ever, the move of the pawn to B-5 was Kasparov's first defensive move that shaped the rest of the game. As for why he refused to take the medication that would treat his condition he explained that when he was hyper it was like the world was in Technicolor, that people around him were moving and thinking in molasses. When he takes the medication it feels like he was dropped down an elevator shaft back into a black and white world. I wish they made a medication that let you down slower and more gentle.

Any thoughts as to the appropriate diagnosis for the three? Let's hop forwards a few years.

Diana is now living in Palm Beach, Florida with a musician who plays for the Boston Pops.
They have a young daughter. Diana is off medication. She feels more complete.

Bob is still living with his parent. His episodes are less severe and further apart.

I received a telephone call from the Sheriff of Union County wondering if I had ever come across a Don XXX. He was scheduled for trial on 7 counts of burglary and one assault. Problem was that every time he's due in court he's always in the hospital.

A solution was reached. Don stood trial and was sentenced to 8-12 years. That was the last emergency call we received regarding Don. It helps when agencies work more closely together.

Bullying and Expectations --

Depression in Adolescence

The world of an adolescent can be a minefield of insecurities. As a child you feel nurture. As an adult you experience autonomy. As a teen you have one foot in the boat and the other on the dock. There is a strong need to belong which can lead to bad choices.

Your body is experiencing eruptions of your complexion and your emotions.
It can be a time in your life when you feel lost, doubting your future and your abilities to shape that future.

If your body shapes to the smaller or weaker or you're just different in belief or social status, you may become a target to the bullying of others seeking to assert their imagined superiority.

Like a cur struck too many times, you may seek to escape life altogether.

And with weapons so easily available you may decide to seek your own imagined superiority if just for a brief moment as you take vengeance against any and all who cross your path. Then you have another Columbine massacre.

Parents -- and even private citizens with no link to a child -- can help prevent school shootings, says Peter Langman, a psychologist and the author of Why Kids Kill: Inside the Minds of School Shooters (Palgrave Macmillan). Here are some of his suggestions:

-- "Set limits on your child's privacy. Keep open communication. Know your child's friends, what he does, what websites he visits. If there is a preoccupation with weapons or violent scenarios in journals, he may need help from a counselor."

-- "Pay attention to school warnings. If the school contacts you with concerns about your child's violent stories or class presentations, he may be depressed or enraged and need help. These 'red flags' have been noticed by teachers before school shootings, but parents rebuffed school officials."

-- "Eliminate easy access to guns at home."

-- "Recognize possible rehearsals of attacks. Some school shooters have done drawings, animations and videos or written stories in advance that depicted brutal acts."

-- "Stay alert to possible signs of future trouble. Private citizens have foiled rampage killings by youths. Among them: a clerk in a photo shop who noticed photos of a teenager with an arsenal of guns and someone who found a notebook with plans for a high school."

Suicide is the third-leading cause of death for 15- to 24-year-olds, according to the Centers for Disease Control and Prevention (CDC), after accidents and homicide. It's also thought that at least 25 attempts are made for every completed teen suicide.

Here is the case of Bobby Smith who lived in South Carolina (real person fake name).

Dan, Bobby's father, is a surgeon who specializes in gastric bypass surgery.

Gastric bypass surgery is the procedure that makes the stomach smaller and allows food to bypass part of the small intestine.

Dan feels that his sons should never settle for second place which presents a bit of a conflict because he has two sons.

Bobby's brother Mike is a year older and is first born and a natural athlete -- which makes it difficult to measure up to.

When Bobby entered the drama club (he had a beautiful singing voice) his father made a snide remark about a bunch of queers and insisted that Bobby try out for a man's sport. Dan was a varsity halfback but had to drop out because of low grades. He was determined that his sons not share his embarrassment.

Bobby has trouble sleeping and is plagued with irritable bowel syndrome that appears resistant to treatment. Dan has a habit of joking about his sons to his friends -- usually when they are with him. To Dan, it's just affectionate pride. Bobby has trouble seeing the humor in Dan's remarks and cringes whenever Dan starts to introduce his sons.

Midterm exams come and Bobby scores a 79 out of 100. He leaves the ceremony and goes to his bedroom. An hour later he takes the family car.

Police say he must have been going in excess of 90 miles an hour when he hit a bridge abutment.

There was an overflow crowd attending Dan's son's funeral.

Recognizing Manipulative People and Controlling Relationships

It's my observation that when you first meet a new acquaintance there is a period of ambivalence. You present your social face as welcoming but in reality you're assessing whether or not to trust this new person in your life. If you like what you see you show your good cards hoping to make a good impression. If not you make whatever excuse you favor to put distance between the two of you.

If the relationship deepens there can be a resistance to letting down an inner wall, again protecting the" ME" from hurt or betrayal or simply from not wanting to expose yourself that quickly in your new relationship.

For whatever reason your emotions allow you to lower the drawbridge to your private face and when that happens there is a warm ebb and flow of personal information exchanged and the feeling that the two of you are now one in spirit.

Of course there is always the neurotic me. It even happens among therapists.

Mary was a social worker in a clinic I worked at in North Carolina. She was a woman in her 40's who had a series of bad marriages. She was a kind Earth Mother who would occasionally show up at work with a black eye or new bruise. One time she didn't show for work for a week taking sick time. She claimed that she tripped and fell down the cellar stairs. That week she filed for divorce.

Six months later she was in love again, a man with a cute nickname, "Hacksaw". She brought him around to meet us. The guy might as well have had a spitting cobra tattooed on his face with a scar running down one cheek and over to the next guy. BAD NEWS. But she was happy.

Some people, I fear, put too much oil on their drawbridge. I think that sociopaths seem to have built in radar that detects the vibrations of an easy and vulnerable mark.

Neurotics need do well enough on their own and don't need the assistance of a sociopath.

However among men there are wolves and foxes. The wolves are more primal and like their cousins of the sea, the shark, their approach is primal.

Then there are the Foxes. These guys are great at seduction. They will say exactly what you want to hear. They will curry and preen your ego and once they catch you turning starry eyes they will start tearing you down, messing with your head and educating you to the fiction that your opinions are naive and only their outlook is valid. Foxes will totally convince you that their farts are a privilege granted.

The key to masculine management is to be alert to your chi. In other words if you go into a room with him and you leave feeling refreshed, alive, valued and confident, then your chi is positive.

On the other hand if you go into a mental space with him and when you leave you feel depressed, insecure, intimidated, confused and worthless -- if you did not bring those emotions INTO the room then you have been manipulated (or outfoxed, if you will).

Manipulation is defined as exerting shrewd or devious influence especially for one's own advantage. The term has something of a negative connotation but it is what it is . . . neither good nor bad. It just is.

When you are faced with the television commercial of a giant digitized cheeseburger with one bite taken out of it shoved in your face and your salivary glands spring into Pavlovian response or when you see a sleep aid commercial with beautiful blue butterflies fanning you asleep while cute little chipmunks cheerfully pull the blanket up to your chin, you've been professionally manipulated.

I construct three types of interactive manipulations:

Manipulation of behavior – trying to get you to do what I want you to do.
Manipulation of emotions – trying to get you to feel the way I want you to feel.
Manipulation of the situation - trying to change the dynamics of the situation.

Manipulation of behavior can work as long as no one catches you at it. Say you are a pretty girl in white gloves who gets a flat tire. You don't want to get hot and sweaty so you stand by the tire, jack in hand, looking confused and helpless. A car pulls up and you say. "The round rubber thingie got all smooshed and I don't know what to do."

The driver smiles and says, "I know you, you're Crash Corrugate. I saw you racing at the Daytona Speedway last Sunday. Rumor has it that you can change a tire in one minute and three seconds."

Caught! Best thing to do is smile admit that you really could use the help and appeal to his better nature.

Manipulation of emotions is usually unfair and counter-productive. Again we take our above-mentioned girl who wakes up filled with energy and ready to jog through the park on such a fine morning. She comes down the stairs and there sits her mother in the one spot of the house where avoiding her is impossible. Her mother gives a weary but heartfelt sigh.

"Mother, what's wrong"?

"Nothing, dear. Have a good time, don't worry about me"?

There were probably many things the girl had on her agenda, jogging through the park, checking the new sales, even pricing the new car she had her eye on. Worrying about Mom just didn't make the list. But then she feels a pang of guilt. Then she feels anger for feeling guilty and guilty for feeling anger after all mother almost died giving birth to you. She has been telling you that on a regular basis whenever she feels her wishes slighted.

Manipulation of emotions: I saw a young fellow who had been dating a girl he was obsessed with. She broke off the relationship because in her mind he was too needy.

His rejoinder to keep her affection? "My brother died, my family hates me. You can't leave; you are all that I've got!" This romantic declaration was as welcome as a gift of a dead mackerel on her lap.

If in your relations with a person you go into a room with a positive feeling but leave with negative guilt or angry feelings you may have been manipulated emotionally. Conversely if every other day you feel angry, offended, betrayed and that others are being unfair, then you may need to see if you are not emotionally manipulating others.

Manipulation of the situation: Here you are trying to influence an outcome -- which is often called "strategy". A football coach devising a playbook to outwit the opposition, or a politician negotiating a compromise are manipulations of the situation. On a more personal, level planning a surprise party . . . same kind of strategy. This is probably the fairest form of manipulation.

So, when you are offered that giant digitized cheeseburger with one bite taken out of it being shoved in your face and your salivary glands springs into Pavlovian response, will you bite the cheeseburger or will the cheeseburger bite you?

Bipolar Thought Disorder --
Thought Disorder In a Bi-Polar
Client's Mind

Saul is a 28 year old single white male who lives with his parents in a nice suburban Tudor styled home. His onset occurred when he was a sophomore in a private college. He has had three hospitalizations.

(Note: I met Saul ... not his real name ... at a computer club. When he learned I was a psychologist he began to sound me out. After awhile he felt comfortable letting me into his perceptions about having a Bi-polar disorder. This is from memory how he shared his insight with me.)

"My name is Saul. I play chess and I'm good at it. I'm ranked as a master. I'm also diagnosed with a disease called Bi-polar. This means there are times when my brain is faster than my body. To be honest, I like the feeling. Hyper means never having to say, you're Saully.

Sorry, I get that way. Language becomes a toy to play with rather than just a way to communicate. But it does bug me that you can have cancer and you only *have* cancer. But with me I don't just *have* bipolar I *am* bipolar I reject that. There are times when I get despondent but it's more likely I feel excitement and the people around me just seem stupid. They say I'm non compliant. I'm naughty. I don't behave. I need my medication they say.

Let me tell you why I don't like to take medicine. When I'm high I feel like everything is explained. That I understand things at the molecular level. My surroundings are in technicolor.

When I get a shot or take the pill my world turns from color to black and white, and I feel like I fell down an elevator shaft. If they would only make a pill that would ease my decompression more slowly. . . .

I do see, I guess, what other people seem to see. When I'm manic the way I talk there are times I talk too fast and stumble over words. I understand what I want to say but my mouth seems unable to shape the words and people say I'm talking too loud. But people are too damn slow and it pisses me off.

That's why I like chess, you can't just jump around like you can in checkers You have to see the boulevard and the alleyways before you make your decision to move.
Shatranj, it was called and they never said "Check mate" it was "Shah Mat". Means "Death to the Shah" in Farsi.

But, you're not a chess player, I can tell. You want to know what it feels like to be bi-polar and why "I'm non compliant. "Compliant, amenable, biddable, obedient, conformable, docile, law-abiding, submissive, tractable". Do I appear docile or submissive to you?

I do take the medicine but it is like what I said before I don't like taking a drug that defines me as being crazy and no matter how you gloss it over that's what it is.

When I feel fine I want to feel more fine and that's when I get into trouble. Because it's a fight. I don't like a drug that controls how I feel. "I know you feel happy but it's not the kind of happy that we have prescribed for you." But if I don't comply I wind up in the hospital, and people know I'm crazy.

But I've learned to live with it. Yet while I know I'm intelligent I'm basically shy around people and not very trusting. Having mental problems will do that to you.

Multiple Personality Disorder

Fact or Fiction?

Albert Hunsticker, during his day, was President of the Illinois Psychological Association. He had an advance degree that exceeded the Ph.D. He was a Diplomat in Clinical psychology. In fact he was on the Board of Examiners for the Diplomat degree. At this level of expertise one would expect the parting of the seas at Galilee or lifting tall buildings with a flicker of thought to be child's play. I was fortunate to have him as a teacher.

One day, six years after the movie "Three Faces of Eve" hit the theaters the subject of Multiple Personality Disorders was brought up in class. Dr. Hunsticker was asked his opinion. With a self deprecating chuckle said, "If in your career you come up with a multiple personality disorder, consider yourself very fortunate and be sure to write a book. Should you come up with two in your career then you have misdiagnosed both of them."

That was 1963. Since then Cris Sizemore (the woman whom the movie was based upon) has had a total of 20 "faces" and has gone on the lecture circuit. I have attended one of her appearances. Multiple Personality Disorder is now called Dissociative Disorder.

However a number of controversies surround dissociative disorder in adults as well as children. First, there is ongoing debate surrounding the etiology of dissociative identity disorder (DID), commonly referred to as multiple personalities. The crux of this debate centers on whether or not DID is the result of childhood trauma or iatrogenesis. Iatrogenesis is defined as "Induced in a patient by a physician's activity, manner, or therapy." (Score one for Dr. Hunsticker).

The Mayo Clinic http://www.mayoclinic.com/health/dissociative-disorders/DS00574 approaches this controversy stating: "We all get lost in a good book or movie. But someone with dissociative disorder escapes reality in ways that are involuntary and unhealthy. The symptoms of dissociative disorders — ranging from amnesia to alternate identities — usually develop as a reaction to trauma and help keep difficult memories at bay."

One of my clients was raped by a black man. This was the South before Roe v. Wade. The procedure was for two clinicians, a psychologist and an MD., to come to an agreement that an abortion was justified. The administrator of the clinic was new so he refused to allow an abortion to occur. This left me with a "where do we go from here" situation.

My client came in for a medication appointment which was difficult as she was in her third trimester. I greeted her and saw that she was very agitated. With an abdomen that had the shape of a watermelon she claimed "Oh, I'm not pregnant, that's my sister, she's the one who's pregnant."

So what is this, Pre partum depression?

Post traumatic stress disorder is also associated with depression and dissociative disorders.

Dr. Matthew Tull is an associate professor and director of anxiety disorders research in the Department of Psychiatry and Human Behavior at the University of Mississippi Medical Center in Jackson contends; "There are several types of dissociative disorders, all of which cause a change in consciousness, memory, identity, or how one views his or her surroundings. This change can come on abruptly or slowly, and it may not happen all the time."

The DSM-IV (Diagnostic and Statistical Manual Forth edition) includes 5 types of dissociative disorders: One of the five is: "Dissociative Identity Disorder: This disorder used to be called, "Multiple Personality Disorder." A person with dissociative identity disorder will have two or more separate identities that each have their own way of thinking and relating to the world. To have this disorder, a minimum of two of these identities must also take control over the person's behavior again and again. Finally, the person with dissociative identity disorder may also have difficulty remembering personal information that, like dissociative amnesia, goes beyond simple forgetfulness."

So what is real and what is chimera? As Fox news is fond of saying,

"We report and you decide."

Suicidal Thoughts and Suicide Decisions

HELP RESOURCES
VA Suicide Hotline: 1-800-273-TALK (8255)
National Suicide Hotline: 1-800-SUICIDE (784-2433)

"It's not that I really want to die, it's just that I will trade it just to be free of the pain I feel."

"I can't face things going right for me, it always turns out bad".

"But that the dread of something after death,
The undiscovered country, from where no traveler
returns, puzzles the will, And makes us rather bear
those ills we have Than fly to others that we know not of?
Thus conscience does make cowards of us all,"
Hamlet

Thoughts of ending your life can be as fleeting as looking down from a tall building and having that flash of thought that makes you back away from the edge. Or it can be sustained such as the feeling that you don't belong and the animosity of your peers seeds rejection and shame.

Tormented thoughts of suicide have plagued Men and Women throughout the ages.

As for successful attempts, the American Association of Suicidology reports that suicide in 2007 was the tenth leading cause of death in the US, accounting for 34,598 deaths. The overall rate was 11.3 suicide deaths per 100,000 people. An estimated 11 attempted suicides occur per every suicide death. And those are the reported attempts for America.1 In fact, as world enonomies worsen, suicide rates in countries around the world are going up.

There is another source of suicides reported that our government would rather you not know. "Since 9/11, more military personnel and veterans have committed suicide than the total dead from both wars in Iraq and Afghanistan combined (total Americans killed in wars = 6,200)3, and this tragedy is occurring despite the best of intentions and programs offered by the Departments of Defense and Veterans Affairs. . . . Still worse is a Centers for Disease Control estimate that 18 veterans from all wars commit suicide every day — that's 6,500 a year!"2 That's a total of around 55,000 vets that have committed suicide since 9/11 . . . a totally shocking number! Our success in teaching young boys to kill is making some finding it hard to live.

Estimates of post-traumatic stress disorder and traumatic brain injury vary widely, but a ballpark figure is that the problems afflict at least one in five veterans from Afghanistan. One study found that by their third or fourth tours in Iraq or Afghanistan, more than one-quarter of soldiers had such mental health problems.

Preliminary figures suggest that being a veteran now roughly doubles one's risk of suicide. For young men ages 17 to 24, being a veteran almost quadruples the risk of suicide, according to a study in The American Journal of Public Health.

An example is a client I treated. Let's call him Joe.

Joe is a former Navy Seal. (SEa Air Land). He is an expert in killing "the enemy". His team saw combat on the Afghan-Pakistan border. On one mission the Intel was totally wrong. They did a HALO jump but landed in a hot zone. They had to fight their way to a landing zone and to safety, but the destination was compromised and when they reached the coordinates they came under mortar fire.

Joe saw a figure attempt to throw a grenade. He rolled and open fire, killing his opponent. It was then he realized he had just murdered a 17 year old girl. What he thought was a grenade was in reality a beanbag.

Attempting to reach the escape helicopter, he was hit in the stomach by a mortar fragment and spent three months in a hospital. He was discharged, but the pictures of the event were seared into his thoughts. He felt the only occupation he was trained for was killing another human being.

When I saw him he was in the throws of PTSD (Post traumatic stress disorder). He was harassing a girl who he heard had a congenital heart disease. He was begging her to take his living heart. It frightened her.

Joe was strong in his belief that he was a murderer and his only salvation was to die in the service of another. He took a job driving an ambulance. His co-workers admired him but didn't want to ride with him. ("Son-of-a-bitch will do crazy shit!"). Movie stunts don't translate well in real life. When I saw him he couldn't sleep and was plagued with flashback. While others saw him as a hero in service for his country, he could only see himself a murderer.

I worked with him for about four months. He still drives like a maniac but at least he is focused on future goals.

Working emergency services including after hours emergency on call I would estimate about 40% are a credible suicide risk. In the time I worked there I did lose one.

The telephone call came in about 9:30pm on a Saturday night. It was a woman who felt her husband was suicidal. When asked for clarification she said that he was drunk and wouldn't stop cleaning his gun. I asked if she tried talking to him and perhaps take possession of the weapon. She elected not to do that. I told her to either take him to the ER or call the police to escort him and I would have the paperwork (for emergency evaluation) ready.

The lethality of the situation speaks to impulsive acting out. He was drunk and he had a gun in his hand. We routinely do not call the police ourselves as there is no way we can assess the lethality of the situation. I received no follow up call from her which was not unusual.

It was Monday before I found out that he killed himself.

Apparently the wife had decided the best option was to gather the children and drive to the church to pray for his soul. While they were at church he shot himself.

While I acknowledge the power of prayer, there is something to be said for the power of common sense.

There is a belief that suicides occur when the victim senses that the family wants to be rid of them. That message seems to have been sent in this case.

My involvement with the police brought me to confront suicides attempts sometimes ongoing and sometimes postmortem.

I was riding with a unit in Charlotte, North Carolina when we received a 10-56 call in a middle class neighborhood. Apparently a white male 37 years of age, divorced, was at his mother-in-law's house with his three children. He was intoxicated and in his bathrobe. The woman had addressed him stating that he needed to get himself together, to stop drinking and go out and find a job. The woman reported that he smiled and replied, "Nah, I'd rather do this." He pulled a revolver and shot himself in the left temple killing himself.

When we arrived we found the children hysterical being comforted rather unsuccessfully by the mother-in-law. The victim was laying on the carpet partially on his left side. The force of the blow-back of the weapon's discharge resulted in fragments of the victim's tongue protruding from the exit wound. Kind of messed his profile.

In my book, **Emergency Services Mental Health Professional - Memoirs and Experiences**, I describe another facet of an impulse attempt:

"About an hour later we received a call from the EMT that a suicide was in progress but the person was refusing treatment. We rolled up; the ambulance was in the driveway its emergency lights painting red swaths on the white wood. Inside was an angry mother, two EMT personnel and a paunchy looking white male in his twenties holding a knife. He had deeply cut his left forearm, blood was streaming so he had cut a vein. Had it been an artery it would have been spurting.

Legally a person has the right to refuse treatment. He was over 21 so his mother couldn't sign papers on him. The blood pooled on the floor as we waited. Most people freak when they see blood. As a point of information loss of blood becomes critical when enough blood is lost that a bath towel becomes saturated.

Snooping a bit I found a handwritten card on the mantle. It was a scribbled note to the boy's father saying that the father was right . . . he was a complete waste and he decided not to bother the family with his presence.

The boy finally fell down unconscious from the blood loss. This was what we were waiting for. He was now in a state of diminished consciousness so not able to make decisions in his own best interest. I nodded and the EMT went to work, packing him up and injecting a saline solution in his arm and transporting him to the ER."

Women don't like guns. As a rule they are more apt to take pills. When a person takes three or five pills I see it as less a suicide and more a cry for attention. Ten or twenty pills they are really trying to check out.

I'm familiar with an actress who depended upon her beauty since she was a child actress. She couldn't face becoming old so she set the stage. She lit candles and put on her favorite sheets and her flowing nightgown. Having established a beautiful memory picture she took a handful of pills.

It didn't go quite as planned. Twenty five minutes later her body is expelling the pills from both ends of her body. She staggered to the bathroom slipped on her vomit and hit the commode with her front teeth and drowned in her own vomit. The National Enquirer has the photo.

I tell this story when I get a client enchanted with the fantasy of a picturesque death.

To me suicide is self murder. If I'm involved I care little about the reason. Kill yourself on your own time not mine.

There are things I look for in a person who is thinking of suicide.

Is the person having trouble concentrating or thinking clearly? Have they set up a situation conducive to impulsive acting out behavior such as standing on a ledge, performing self-destructive behaviors, such as heavily drinking alcohol, using illegal drugs, or cutting their body?

By contrast is the person creating an organized attempt such as giving away belongings or talking about going away or the need to "get my affairs in order."Are they giving a signal that they are retreating from social interacting such as losing interest in activities that they used to enjoy? A sudden change of behavior, especially calmness after a period of anxiety, losing interest in activities that they used to enjoy, pulling away from friends or not wanting to go out.

Talking about death or suicide, or even saying that they want to hurt themselves, feeling hopeless or guilty, major change in sleep or eating habits, talking about feeling hopeless or guilty are all strong warning signs of an attempted suicide.

While you might think that killing yourself is relatively easy. I had a girl who had a surefire attempt, in more ways than one. She took off her clothes and sat in the bathtub so as to contain the mess. She placed a double barreled shotgun to her abdomen and pulled both barrels. She lived. But not without a lot of internal damage that in no uncertain terms she had to live with.

When I'm on the phone and I don't know the person or his or her intent. I listen for any clue to their history and back ground. I want to know how religious they are. As Shakespeare's Hamlet intones "But that the dread of something after death, The undiscovered country, from where No traveler returns, puzzles the will".

I try to see if they still have any sense of humor left. If we can laugh, no matter how dark, there is a spark left.

My primary goal is to establish something that the person might be looking forwards to. It can even be as mundane as a favorite television show. I try to reinforce that "I understand that you want to kill yourself but why be in such a hurry. Let's meet first. We have established that we both (blank). You can always kill yourself any time, let's do this first."

I'm looking for a promise and the longer we talk the more likely I'll be able to get that promise.

If I get a hang-up I have a device that tells me where the call came from. My next call is to 911. Sirens and flashing lights tend to embarrass the neighborhood. Thankfully I've never had to use it.

Death is the one thing no matter how clumsy you are you will get right the first time. You really don't need practice sessions.

References

1 -- http://www.nimh.nih.gov/health/publications/suicide-in-the-us-statistics-and-prevention/index.shtml

2 -- http://www.vfw.org/News-and-Events/Articles/VFW-Stands-Up-Against-Military-Suicides/

3 -- http://www.msnbc.msn.com/id/44777299/ns/us_news-life/t/one-in-three-vets-say-iraq-afghan-wars-were-not-worth-it/#.T42bdNnv7Kg

Suicide in the Elderly

Problems of Aging, Statistics, and a Meaningful Life

"Grow old along with me! The best is yet to be"

That's all well and good but when you get up and its hard to walk without supporting yourself you kinda wonder, "How old was the fool who wrote those words? "

When you look back at who you were and what you could do then that you can't do now it can get kind of discouraging.

The children are grown and have moved on except when they drop back with a load of laundry to get done. Then there are neighbors who have lost their spouse, have a chronic illness or just feel useless. In the minds of some is the feeling "why should I keep on?"

Some don't.

The National Institute of Mental Health reports there is one elderly suicide every 97 minutes. There are about 14.9 elderly suicides each day, resulting in 5,421 suicides among those 65 and older.

Elderly white men are at the highest risk with a rate of approximately 31.1 suicides per 100,000 each year. White men over the age of 85, who are labeled "old-old", were at the greatest risk of all; the suicide rate for these men was 45.42 per 100,000. That is 2.5 times the current rate for men of all ages (18.3 per 100,000). 84.4% of elderly suicides are male; the rate of male suicides in late life is 7.3 times greater than for female suicides.

The death of one is a tragedy . . . . the death of many? . . . just a statistic.

Consider Dave, diagnosed with A.L.S. He first noted a weakness in his right hand that spread to his legs. A few months later it progressed. He experienced a generalized clumsiness, stiff walking with overwhelming fatigue. It was then he felt panic as he felt difficulty swallowing or breathing, with muscle cramps during the night. He took stock of his future. Pretty soon he will not be able to care for himself. The burden will fall on his wife and whatever insurance he has left.

He has a long discussion with his wife. She doesn't like it but will accept her husband's decision. He fills the tub with hot water and with his wife holding his hand he kills himself.

Had I been on call I would be honor bound to rescue him. What exactly would I be rescuing him from?

Let's look at the flip side of this coin, another story, this one with less gloom and doom. It has to do with Mary. She was living in a retirement home and was very popular with the other residents -- some of it due in part to her notoriety, She was a can can dancer during the Alaskan gold rush of 1898. Her observation on her life? She said "No one really regrets the journey one takes. It was those who feared taking that journey that regretted their inaction."

There is a line in Meredith Willson's "The Music Man" that underscores Mary's observation; "If you wait for too many tomorrows all you will have is a handful of empty yesterdays".

That, my readers, is a significant clue to a satisfying life.

There is a place in Florida called Century Village. It was the brain child of comedian/actor Red Buttons. It was creatively laid out with apartment buildings, duplexes, family homes; structures familiar to the types of homes its occupants were familiar with how they used to live.

Every week they brought in acts or groups to entertain the residents; a Yiddish comedian for the city folks or square dancing for the suburban crowds.

As a consultant to United Way's Retired Senior Volunteer Program (RSVP). I got into a conversation with one of their residents. He made an astute observation. He said, "I'm really grateful for what they do for us. I just wish, someday they would ask something from us."

The purpose of RSVP is to draw upon the talents of seniors who volunteer to help others. And that is another important clue to a fulfilling life and a means for combating depression.

Get out of your house and get out of your problems and devote part of your day to helping others.

Second, watch what you eat. Our diet usually consists of too much fat, too much meat, too much salt, too many calories, and too much fast food. Not only do we eat the wrong kinds of food, but we also eat far too much at mealtime.

You have to begin sometime so make today the day you begin a healthier life.

Third get off your butt and engage in age appropriate exercise. That doesn't mean entering the local Tough Man contest or being a participant in the Boston Marathon. It does mean attending to movement, balance, blood pressure and breathing.

Third be an active participant in your own health needs. Sometimes doctors prescribe medicine to treat a certain condition not realizing that as you grow older that what you are taking can contribute to over-medication.

As you grow past retirement you might want to consider a physician who specializes in geriatric medicine.

According to Gail Sullivan, a professor at the UConn School of Medicine and associate director for education at the Center on Aging. fewer than 1 percent of all physicians in the country are certified in geriatric medication and treatment.

What are the common symptoms of elderly patients who are over-medicated?

• Fatigue
• Motor problems such as walking and standing
• Skin flushing and rashes

- Weight loss or gain
- Falling and problems with balance
- Mood swings
- Changes in personal hygiene
- Physical impairment
- Memory problems
- Hallucinations both visual and auditory
- Confusion
- Thinking and reasoning problems
- Abdominal pain

. . . symptoms that are easily confused with other psychiatric diagnosis.

Finally, get involved with your world. In the last presidential election, nationally at least 79 % of those 65 and older cast ballots. This is compared to an overall voter turnout of 52 percent, according to the U.S. Census Bureau.

You're retired so you have time. Learn about the different candidates in your town and on the national stage and keep in mind the different issues that affect your life and that of your family.

You are not just voting for one man, the president, Rather you are voting for a group of men and women who will be taking over the country and making decisions in your best interest – or, unfortunately, in their best interest. Be wary of bumper sticker solutions or "swift boating" a candidate's character or abilities. Whether you win or lose it will help you to be aware of the world around you, how it works and how it affects the quality of your life.

I complain that the years fly past, but then I look in a mirror and see that very few of them actually got past. ~Robert Brault

We are always the same age inside. ~Gertrude Stein

Depression and the Famous

Actors. Politicians. Writers. No One's Immune.

Feeling a little depressed or for that matter do you feel an emptiness like depression is overwhelming you?

Alone in a prison of your own making? It's a lonely world isn't it? Actually you have a lot of company. Maybe, just maybe it may be a sign of creativity.

You have probably heard of Winston Churchill and his depression which he called his "Black Dog." You may have even heard that Newsman Mike Wallace almost committed suicide. It was during a time where he was sued by General Westmoreland for a story Mike did on the Vietnam war. BTW Mike was proven to be accurate.

There are others you might not have guessed. Let me share some of their stories.

How about Rodney Dangerfield, you know the comedian, " "I don't get no respect!," "No respect, no respect at all... that's the story of my life" Not his real name by the way it's Jacob Cohen.

He began to perform at the age of 20 under the name Jack Roy. Tried it for nine years without success. He tried his luck as a singing waiter until he was fired, and also working as a performing acrobatic diver before giving up show business to take a job selling aluminum siding to support his wife and family. That would depress anyone. The name Rodney Dangerfield was a fictitious character from the old Jack Benny show. And like Benny he developed a character who was the perpetual loser. When asked his real name he insisted it was Percival Sweetwater.

Actress Catherine Zeta-Jones checked into a Connecticut mental health facility to be treated for bipolar II disorder, which is characterized by swings between depression and hypomania.

The actress Gwyneth Paltrow revealed the postpostpartum depression she experienced in a 2008 interview with Vogue. J.K. Rowling the creator of Harry Potter living as a single mother in a cramped apartment after separating from her first husband, J.K. Rowling suffered from suicidal thoughts and underwent cognitive behavioral therapy. She claims that the Dementors (the dark hooded creatures in "Harry Potter and The Prisoner Of Azkaban" who detect their victims' secret fears and then suck out their personalities) were based on her experience with depression.

Project Runway's Tim Gunn is the epitome of style. As a 17-year-old struggling with his sexuality, Gunn took more than 100 pills in a suicide attempt.

In a recent video for The Trevor Project, a national organization that aims to prevent crisis and suicide among gay and lesbian youth, Gunn explained, "I'm very happy today that that attempt was unsuccessful, but at the time it's all that I could contemplate."

He said he wants everyone who's feeling hopeless to know that "it gets better; it really does."

Peanuts creator Charles Schulz poured his depression into his comics, making Charlie Brown a sort of Everyman. After his death in 2000, Time quoted a friend saying, "I think that one of the things that afforded [him] his greatness was his unwillingness to turn his back on the pain."

Schulz took refuge in his comic strip and hoped it would give readers that same escape from their own everyday struggles.

One of the happiest seeming celebrity would be Ellen DeGeneres. The media frenzy caused by Ellen coming out in 1997 caused her to be mired in depression for three years. The controversy also reportedly put pressure on her relationship with then-girlfriend, Anne Heche, as well as contributed to the cancellation of her sitcom, Ellen. Rebounding with a vengeance, the talk show queen, now 52, currently is enjoying the success of a lifetime and is happily married to her longtime girlfriend, Portia de Rossi.

When you chose an alternative lifestyle you are going to bump into critics of your choices and their rejection and scorn is going to hurt.

As a performer your very livelihood is dependent upon the approval of the general public. Doubts of one's own abilities when it is those abilities that sustain your survival open the door to depression and self loathing.

As a psychologist I'm familiar with some of the histories I've reported. As for the rest a couple of evening curled up with Google opens the door to other discoveries. You would be surprised how many truly great people live lives of quiet desperation. I could go on but so can you. Look up the lives of:

Charles Dickens
Fyodor Dostoyevsky
Tchaikovsky
Abraham Lincoln
Edgar Allan Poe
Boris Yeltsin
Hans Christian Andersen
Astronaut Buzz Aldrin
William Faulkner
Ernest Hemingway
Hamid Karzai (President of Afghanistan)
Richard Nixon
Sir Isaac Newton
John D Rockefeller
Oprah Winfrey

These actors, artists, world leaders and authors were able to accomplish great things despite their struggles with the disease.

If they can, so can you.

Trapped in the prison of your own depression what goes on in the lives of others is irrelevant to your own sorrows. Yet they left the dark woods and and entered the clearing. It is said the depression is anger turned inwards.

When you feel down maybe this saying bares constant repeating; "I may not be much but I'm all that I've got so let me treat myself with the same respect that I afford others." (That's only fair isn't it?)

Try it.

How to Help Someone With Depression

Editor's Note: Friends and family can be very helpful for someone experiencing the lows of a depression but in order for them to know HOW to help I asked our guest author and experienced psychologist of 45 years to give us a few tips.

###

When a psychiatrist views the dis-ease of depression they frequently link it with anxiety as if it were the same illness. Tagging along behind is an emotion called "worry". Let's herd them into separate pens and give them a closer look before we brand them.

First let's examine the critter called "worry" Under a cold hard stare we can strip it of its outer covering and see it for what it is. Worry is nothing more and nothing less than negative fantasy. A fantasy of everything that could go wrong will go wrong. Worry in the short term can be helpful "Did I leave the water running?". To satisfy this worry you check to see if the faucets are turned off and you go on with your life. But for some worry is an addiction. The person becomes so consumed with worry that it freezes the will from any decisive action.

A close side running partner to worry is "anxiety". What's the difference between the two? With worry you are mentally stuck in the past. With anxiety you are mentally stuck in the future. Let me give an example.

You are facing a big chemistry mid-term. exam You are anxious that you won't do well, that you haven't studied hard enough, and even if you did What would a failing grade do to your other subjects.

So you take the exam and lo and behold you flopped it, big time. Now you are no longer anxious you're sad and worried. You don't feel anxious about the test now you just feel regret that it happened the way it did. Suddenly you feel anxious again. Will you flunk out of college? What will your parents say? Will you have to go to work? What kind of job will you be able to get?

By now you are probably aware of the difference between situational depression, you flunked out of school and feel sad about it, as opposed to Clinical depression, you feel profoundly sad without any obvious reason. Things may be going well for you but this dark wave of sadness washes over you....and stays.

A doctor would explain that the patient's level of serotonin was too low. Serotonin is primarily found in the gastrointestinal (GI) tract, platelets, and in the central nervous system (CNS) of animals including the gastroenteritis of humans. It is popularly thought to be a contributor to feelings of well-being and happiness.

Which only goes to show you really need guts to overcome depression.

So you would like to help someone who is depressed.

First you need to take a reading of whether your friend even wants your involvement. You can let your friend know that if he or she wants to vent that you will be there for them. Wait a heartbeat or two to see if the slats open. if it doesn't you have shown your willingness to help.

If your friend does vent then listen, understand but do not pass judgment. And for heaven's sake keep your slats closed; don't you start venting. It should not be a contest of "Nobody knows the trouble I've seen." -- and don't try to fix it with unsolicited advice like ""Have you tried aromatherapy? There was an article about it in the paper…" . This kind of comment can come across as trivializing your friend's concerns. Just let your friend know you are on their side and let him have his say.

Be there but also realize your friend has arrived with a monkey on their back. When they leave the monkey goes with them.

While it is important to accept the person in the state they are in, don't let it totally consume your life. Otherwise, you'll fall in a heap and won't be much help to anyone. You need to take care of yourself. "I am committed to you and to helping you. But I also need to eat / shop / go out for coffee / ring a friend / see a movie to recharge my batteries. Then I can look after you better."

"We don't see things the way they are. We see them the way WE are." – Talmud.

"The reason people find it so hard to be happy is that they always see the past better than it was, the present worse than it is, and the future less resolved than it will be." – Marcel Pagnol

###

If you found these case studies interesting or helpful, please consider checking out Jack's book. You'll find more of his sage advice there.

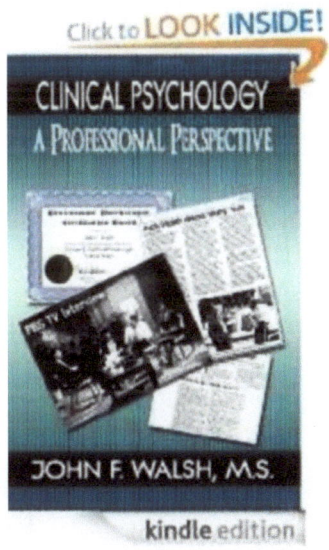

EXCERPT from _Clinical Psychology: a Professional Perspective_

CHAPTER 8 What About Me?

Every now and then, I'm asked to speak to a group or a class.

During one class of advanced-education psychology students, I mentioned Sigmund Freud. No one in the class ever heard of him. I thought they were putting me on. I mean, come on now, Freud? You know ... the fuzz-faced dude who got cancer of the jaw from smoking too many stogies. The guy who could have discovered local anesthesia had he not been getting down with some chick when another dude named Carl Koller beat him to the punch? That guy. Oh, he also reported his construct of the "id", "ego" and "super ego".

Of course, we're not talking about things or places, but a process or a description of a mental state. I still have people come up to me and say, "You believe in that 'unconscious' stuff?" To my unconsciously deprived friend, I asked how he got here. He replied, "I walked here".

Hmm... did you start out with your right foot or your left foot?" What is your estimate of the distance between one foot and the other? When you reached for the doorknob, did you turn it clockwise or counterclockwise? Was each of these activities meticulously planned ahead of time or did you just do it? If so, how? "Unconsciousness" does have a habit of sneaking up on you.

Psychological theories are sort of like mental coat racks to hang various constructs upon. There are various constructs used to explain how we became the way we are. Karen Horney describes neurotic perceptions as "a child lost and lonely in a potentially hostile world". As a result, one makes the choice to move toward, move against or move away.

Here are some definitions:

Moving Toward People: the person's need for affection and approval; pleasing others and being liked by them.

Moving Against People: the person's need for power; the ability to force or manipulate people in order to achieve control over others.

Moving Away from People: the need for avoidance by means of withdrawal, perfectionism (denying any flaws) or social invisibility.

Horney describes the difference between a healthy person and a neurotic person as: "the healthy person has a realistic appraisal of their strengths and weaknesses and has the ability to build on those strengths and abilities, while the neurotic is trapped fighting the windmills of their own makings".

My own construct, a word picture that I use with clients to describe a person's neurotic self concept is "the presence of me". It is the tiny core that is the person we see in the mirror, but through a distorted lens. If > > me < < is so tiny, vulnerable and helpless, we need to protect it with a wall to keep our feelings from being hurt. But maybe the wall isn't strong enough, so we had better develop spikes to protect the walls. And, if even that is not enough, we will build a sturdier, thicker wall beyond the spikes in order to protect the vulnerable > > me < <. In doing so, we have constructed an impenetrable fortress to protect ones feelings from being hurt. The problem is, with a fortress so strong we have inadvertently built a prison, one in which we are trapped.

As one client put it, "We hide ourselves from ourselves. Then we go to protect ourselves, but where do we begin?" There is a healthier alternative...
There's me again. "Me!" may not be much, but I'm all that I have, so why not accept Me for who I am. Of course, there may be things I choose not to share with you, like my mother is in the witness protection program or that I have an obsessive need to shove macadamia nuts up my nose. But the rest of me is approachable.

Again, going back to Karen Horney, she believed that if one has an accurate conception of oneself, then one is free to realize one's potential and achieve what one wishes -- within reasonable boundaries. Thus, she believed that "self-actualization" (a term coined by Herbert Maslow, meaning pretty much the same thing) is the healthy person's aim through life -- as opposed to the neurotic's clinging to a set of key needs.

It's my observation that when you first meet a new acquaintance, there is a period of ambivalence. You present your social face as welcoming but continue to assess whether or not to trust this new person in your life. If you
like what you see, you show your good cards, hoping to make a good impression. If not, you make whatever excuse you favor to put distance between the two of you.

If the relationship deepens, there can be a resistance to letting down an inner wall, again protecting the ME from hurt or betrayal or simply from not wanting to expose yourself that quickly in your relationship. For whatever reason, your emotions allow you to lower the drawbridge to your private face. When that happens, there is a warm ebb and flow of personal information exchanged and the feeling that the two of you are now one, in spirit.

Of course, there is always the neurotic "me". It even happens among therapists. Mary was a social worker in a clinic I worked at in North Carolina. She was a woman in her 40' s who had a series of bad marriages. She was a kind Earth Mother who would occasionally show up at work with a black eye or a new bruise. One time, she didn't show up for work for a week, taking sick time. She claimed that she tripped and fell down the cellar stairs. That week she filed for divorce.

Six months later, she was in love again with a man with a cute nickname: "Hacksaw". She brought him around to meet us. The guy might as well have had a spitting cobra tattooed on his face with a scar running down one cheek and over to the next guy. He was BAD NEWS, but she was happy.

Some people, I fear, put too much oil on their drawbridge. I think that sociopaths seem to have built-in radar that detects the vibrations of an easy and vulnerable mark. Neurotics do well enough on their own and don't need the assistance of a sociopath.

Manipulation is defined as exerting shrewd or devious influence, especially for one's own advantage. The term has something of a negative connotation, but it is what it is -- neither good nor bad. It just is.

When you are faced with the television commercial of a giant, digitized cheeseburger with one bite taken out of it shoved in your face and your salivary glands spring into a Pavlovian response, or when you see a sleep aid commercial with beautiful blue butterflies fanning you asleep, while cute little chipmunks cheerfully pull the blanket up to your chin, you've been professionally manipulated.

I construct three types of interactive manipulations:

Manipulation of behavior – trying to get you to do what I want you to do.

Manipulation of emotions – trying to get you to feel the way I want you to feel.

Manipulation of the situation - trying to change the dynamics of the situation.

Manipulation of behavior can work as long as no one catches you at it. Say you are a pretty girl in white gloves who gets a flat tire. You don't want to get hot and sweaty, so you stand by the tire, jack in hand, looking confused and helpless. A car pulls up and you say, "The round rubber thing got all smooshed and I don't know what to do." The driver smiles and says, "I know you, you're Crash Corrugate. I saw you racing at the Daytona Speedway last Sunday. Rumor has it that you can change a tire in one minute and three seconds". Caught! The best thing to do is smile, admit that you really could use the help and appeal to his better nature.

Manipulation of emotions is usually unfair and counterproductive. Again, we take our above-mentioned girl, who wakes up filled with energy and ready to jog through the park on such a fine morning. She comes down the stairs and there sits her mother in the one spot of the house where avoiding her is impossible. Her mother gives a weary, but heartfelt, sigh. "Mother, what's wrong"? "Nothing, dear. Have a good time and don't worry about me". There were probably many things the girl had on her agenda, such as jogging through the park, checking the new sales, even pricing the new car she had her eye on. Worrying about Mom just did not make the list, but then she feels a pang of guilt. Then, she feels anger for feeling guilty and guilty for feeling anger. After all, mother almost died giving birth to you. She has been telling you that, on a regular basis, whenever she feels her wishes slighted.

Manipulation of emotions: I saw a young fellow who had been dating a girl he was obsessed with. She broke off the relationship because, in her mind, he was too needy. His rejoinder to keep her affection? "My brother died; my family hates me; you can't leave; you're all I have!" This romantic declaration was as welcome as a gift of a dead mackerel on her lap. If, in your relations with a person, you go into a room with a positive feeling, but leave with negative guilt or angry feelings, you may have been manipulated emotionally. Conversely, if every other day you feel angry, offended, betrayed and that others are being unfair, then you may need to see if you are not emotionally manipulating others.

Manipulation of the situation: Here you are trying to influence an outcome. Often, it is called "strategy". A football coach devising a playbook to outwit the opposition, or a politician negotiating a compromise, are manipulating the situation. On a more personal level, planning a surprise party is the same kind of strategy. This is probably the fairest form of manipulation.

# # #

To check out Jack's book, just copy and paste this link into your search bar.
http://www.amazon.com/dp/B0088QWH8Q

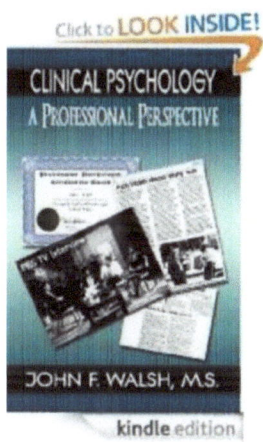

To brouse books by Joyce Zborower, go to Amazon.com and type her name into Amazon search bar.

If you are dealing with any type of depression, or you think you are, it's important to know you're not alone. Millions of people just like you experience the signs and symptoms of depression and begin treatment. The good news is that depression is treatable. With the right treatment plan, you can begin to climb out of the hole.

Thank you for purchasing **How to Fight Depression – 9 case studies** ---- by John F. Walsh. If you enjoyed it or found it useful, would you take a few minutes and write a short review on its Amazon page? Also, please let your friends know about it on Facebook and Twitter. If it makes a difference in their lives, they will thank you. As will I.

Best wishes,
Joyce Zborower